Strategies and Tips for Paralegal Educators

Anita Tebbe
Johnson County Community College

West Publishing Company

Minneapolis/St. Paul   New York   Los Angeles   San Francisco

WEST'S COMMITMENT TO THE ENVIRONMENT

In 1906, West Publishing Company began recycling materials left over from the production of books. This began a tradition of efficient and responsible use of resources. Today, up to 95% of our legal books and 70% of our college texts and school texts are printed on recycled, acid-free stock. West also recycles nearly 22 million pounds of scrap paper annually—the equivalent of 181,717 trees. Since the 1960s, West has devised ways to capture and recycle waste inks, solvents, oils, and vapors created in the printing process. We also recycle plastics of all kinds, wood, glass, corrugated cardboard, and batteries, and have eliminated the use of Styrofoam book packaging. We at West are proud of the longevity and the scope of our commitment to the environment.

Production, Prepress, Printing and Binding by West Publishing Company.

 TEXT IS PRINTED ON 10% POST CONSUMER RECYCLED PAPER    PRINTED WITH **SOY INK**

CONTENTS

CHAPTER ONE

The WHO of Paralegal Education
Teachers and Students

The *Human* Factor

Take a dedicated teacher and motivated students, mix with a solid paralegal curriculum, and you have successful education. It is so simple, but
challenging!

What do you recall when you think of your "good, ole days" as a student:
mastering difficult concepts, paging through dusty library books, or cram-
ming for those mid-terms? Or perhaps you recall a demanding high
school journalism teacher who treated you as an unique individual, or an
absent-minded but brilliant college Russian history instructor, who
encouraged you to pursue graduate studies, or a friendly property law pro-
fessor, who frequently asked about your family. Education is a *human*
endeavor: People encouraging people to believe in themselves and people
helping others understand that "only the educated are free."

A key human component of this noble profession is the *teacher*. In paralegal education, these significant people are often practicing lawyers and
legal assistants, who relate their valuable experience to students through
classroom instruction. What a gold mine: attorneys and legal assistants,
who are willing to share their expertise with paralegal students.

1

Selection of the best person for a paralegal position is an important task. It is helpful if the applicant possesses three qualities: 1) mastery of course content and awareness of its application in today's workplace; 2) ability to communicate knowledge and demonstrate skills, and 3) comprehension of essential information concerning the paralegal profession and legal issues that influence education.

Subject Matter

Knowledge of subject matter is the foundation of successful teaching. To assure this requirement is met, an instructor must be well-informed. To keep up-to-date in a particular area, a teacher should stay well-read, attend conferences and discuss pertinent issues with colleagues. (A bonus for any teacher, especially an inexperienced one, is to be assigned a mentor.) Possessing omniscient traits, however, is not a prerequisite for an educator. There is nothing wrong in saying the three words, "I don't know," if the situation arises.

For some paralegal instructors, their last formal education was on the graduate level, where some professors were "long on theory and short on application." Also, a few of these academicians presented material by boring lectures, a way to "exhibit their erudition." To avoid these tendencies, legal assistant teachers need to balance their instruction with a discussion of the *what* and *how* of law through interactive teaching.

Applied learning is an important component of paralegal classes. The instructor can provide hands-on training through practical class activities, like document-drafting or mock interviews. A Chinese saying reflects this attitude, "give a man a fish and you feed him for a day. Teach a man to fish and you feed him for a lifetime."

Methodology

In education, it is important to have something to say. What to teach, however, must be coupled with knowing HOW TO TEACH. Among the qualities that assure effectiveness in a classroom are preparation, organization, enthusiasm, and humor.

The management principles of W. Edwards Deming have influenced education through the Total Quality Management movement. Accountability must be a component of education. This awesome responsibility of teaching is fulfilled if we follow the Boy Scout motto, "Be Prepared." Good class presentations are the result of careful and thorough planning. To share "war stories" has a place but should be used sparingly and certainly not be a time-filler for inadequate preparation.

Teachers should also avoid using class time to read extensive textbook passages or other material to students. This technique is a time waster and raises questions concerning adequate teacher preparation.

Organization/Order/Pace

Organization is needed in order to effectively present material. Do you ever recall an incident like this one: You dash into class late and look like you just survived a Kansas tornado. You drop your book on the desk and say, "Now, where did we leave off?"

To guarantee that an instructor knows where to start and how to stay on point, an *outline* of the lesson's major points can be presented at the beginning of each class. This overview can be shared by putting it on the board, displaying it by means of an overhead transparency, or giving individual hand-outs to students. As the class progresses, students can be encouraged to amplify the outline by taking additional notes. (A sample outline is included in Appendix I.)

Another indication of good organization is to start and end class on time. Prompt collection and return of assignments are also important and returned papers should have explanatory remarks rather than just a letter or number grade.

To assist in good organization, the order and pace of a presentation are important. Learning is distributive, connecting earlier concepts with new ideas. An example of this bridging approach is: "Last class we discussed jurisdiction, the authority of a court to hear a case. Today we are going to take the idea a step further and discuss the concept of venue, that is, which particular court within the federal or state court systems will hear the case, once jurisdiction has been established."

While many instructors worry about the problem of "so much content and so little time," pacing of material is an important component of successful teaching. Repetition is critical. When stressing a crucial point, teachers can preface their remarks with statements like, "is everyone listening;" or "this is probably important because it is the third time I have said it today"; or even "I bet you are going to be fortunate enough to see this matter addressed on the next test." Each major point should be illustrated with a clear explanation and concrete example. A common misconception is that an idea is understood by going over it one time. Important concepts should be repeated in a spiral method rather than a linear approach. *Covering material is not teaching.*

Enthusiasm

A quality of an excellent teacher is <u>enthusiasm</u>. Before going into a class-room, it helps to recall how fortunate one is to be involved in this privi-leged profession. As a Chinese philosopher wisely observed many years ago,

> If you plan for a year, plant a seed.
> If for ten years, plant a tree.
> If for a hundred years, teach the people.
> (Kuan Chung)

To contemplate this same powerful idea in more contemporary terms, one can paraphrase the commercial, "care enough to send the best," with the variation, "care enough to do your best." While the saying, "life is just one long vacation to people who love their work," is an interesting idea, this positive spirit should certainly be a distinguishing characteristic of educators.

Humor

If educators do not convey a positive attitude about teaching, students are short-changed. An up-beat attitude is reflected by the teacher's energy and humor. Life, either inside or outside the "ivory" tower, is to be enjoyed, not just tolerated. To be able to laugh <u>at oneself</u> and laugh <u>with students,</u> (never at students), are refreshing qualities.

Paralegal Profession

Knowledge of several areas will help a paralegal instructor be a more effective teacher. General understanding of the paralegal profession will improve the instructor's impact, such as:

- ⊗ the profession's history,
- ⊗ current and controversial matters facing paralegals (regulation, legal technicians,....),
- ⊗ major national/state/local paralegal organizations,
- ⊗ types of paralegal programs,
- ⊗ the American Bar Association approval process,
- ⊗ paralegal employment opportunities, and
- ⊗ the professional organization, American Association for Paralegal Education. (Membership in the American Association for Paralegal Education provides many opportunities to keep up-to-date on education matters. The bimonthly magazine, Legal Assistant Today, is also an excellent source for current developments in the paralegal profession.)

Instructors should understand *paralegal ethical issues*. Some important topics today are concerned with conflict of interest, confidentiality, and unauthorized practice of law. While some of these issues are gray areas, it is important to raise the student's consciousness of potential problems. Discussion of ethical issues should be a fundamental part of every course. "To educate a man in mind and not in morals is to educate a menace to society." (Theodore Roosevelt)

Legal Issues

While it seems unnecessary to remind attorney and paralegal educators to be aware of important legal issues, these laws can be complicated. The Buckley Amendment (The Federal Educational Rights and Privacy Act), Copyrights Act, and Discrimination Laws, especially Americans with Disabilities Act, are significant pieces of legislation.

Buckley Amendment

The <u>Buckley Amendment</u> states that student information, such as address, phone number, grades, and class attendance, is to be kept in confidence and not released to third parties unless the student gives consent. The guidelines only apply to people outside the educational institution and does not affect the reporting of grades and attendance for internal purposes. Some schools have applied this Amendment with specific directives: 1) grades should not be posted; 2) academic work should not be left in a public access area for students to pick up; 3) a course schedule of a student should not be released; and 4) inquiries about a student's attendance, class progress or grades should not be given.

Copyrights Act

Another important law is the <u>Copyrights Act</u>. Section 106 describes the exclusive rights of copyright owners. Section 107 establishes four basic factors to be examined in determining the "fair use" provision under the copyright law. These considerations are:

⊗ the purpose of use, including whether for non-profit educational purposes,

⊗ the nature of the copyrighted work,

⊗ the amount of the work used in relation to the copyrighted work, and

⊗ the effect of the use upon the potential market for the copyrighted work.

(To obtain further information on this important law, refer to Questions and Answers on Copyright for the Campus Community, a 1993 publication by National Association of College Stores, Inc. and The Association of American Publishers.)

Discrimination Laws/Americans with Disabilities Act
Teachers should avoid even the perception of bias and should attempt to use ethnic-varied fact patterns and gender-neutral language. Specifically, instructors need to understand the recent civil rights law, Americans with Disabilities Act. This law provides comprehensive protection for people with special needs. A public institution must make reasonable modifications in policies and practices in order to assist disabled individuals.

Policies and Procedures

Finally, once teachers are hired, it is critical that they know and follow administrative procedures of the school and paralegal program. Some important policies are concerned with

⊗ class cancellations,

⊗ room changes,

⊗ grade changes,

⊗ instructor's absence,

⊗ attendance and grade records,

⊗ guest speakers,

⊗ textbooks,

⊗ field trips, and

⊗ equipment use.

The instructor should also be aware of ancillary services on campus for teachers and students, such as a writing center, tutors, computer-assisted legal research terminals, career counselors, and multimedia center.

Student-Centered Approach

Paralegal teachers must possess sound pedagogical principles and also remember that education is a people-to-people profession. The focus must always be on the student.

A cardinal educational precept is "to take students from where they are to where they need to be." To apply this principle to today's paralegal programs is especially challenging because of the heterogeneous student population. Class composition is often diverse in regard to range of ages, span of abilities, differences of educational backgrounds, and variance of socio-cultural experiences.

Teachers need to appreciate this diversity. To promote appropriate group dynamics among students, instructors need to be aware of a possible class split according to the age factor: a generational barrier between traditional and non-traditional students.

Traditional students are college-age students ranging from 18 to 25 years. While they realize the value of higher education, they possess limited life experience. However, they are perceptive enough to realize that life is challenging and even harder if one is uneducated. While it is dangerous to stereotype, some traits often found with the younger population are passive learners, linear thinkers with a black and white approach to problem-solving and preference for anonymity in an educational setting. In contrast, the over 25 year old students, the non-traditional students, are often second career persons, struggling to balance job and family responsibilities. They desire recognition and individual acknowledgement, are motivated, but apprehensive about returning to school.

Respect

The challenge of the paralegal instructor is to welcome the diverse situational aspect of each class. The best way to deal with an individual is to treat him/her with a respectful attitude. In practical terms, some suggestions are to

- ⊗ learn students' names,
- ⊗ set a goal to discover something new about a different student each class, (through conversations at breaks or before/after class),
- ⊗ encourage each person to participate in class and reinforce students' contributions with positive comments,
- ⊗ allow students to share life experiences that are relevant to class, (these examples are like a teacher's "war stories"; they are valuable if sprinkled sparingly and are not too personal in nature), and
- ⊗ acknowledge out-of-class accomplishments of students in class, such as publishing an article in the school

newspaper or winning a scholarship.

If the Golden Rule is practiced in a classroom, a person's best traits surface. Respect engenders respect.

Realistically, how does a teacher deal with the rare problem student: the talkative and/or argumentative person. During class discussions, some students seem to like to hear themselves talk. The instructor needs to affirm the value of each person's insights but should change the classroom dynamics by calling on other students for various viewpoints. In regard to an occasional student who likes to converse when another person is talking, the teacher should have all discussion stop except the individual speaking out-of-turn. The ensuing silence is a powerful way for everyone to understand the need for common courtesy.

An argumentative person can be challenging, too. The instructor can often prevent escalating tension by acknowledging an individual's right to different opinions. If the behavior persists, the instructor should suggest that the individual meet outside class time to discuss the matter in greater detail.

If any of these situations occur, the instructor must act in a firm manner. While it sounds simplistic, many classroom problems can be prevented by a teacher's insistence on mutual respect -- this atmosphere is so disarming!

CHAPTER TWO

The WHAT of Paralegal Education
Subject Matter

How Much Do I Need to Know?

How much educational theory do teachers need to know before they can confidently enter a classroom? Shouldn't teaching be like the no-nonsense approach of " 'Begin at the beginning,' the king said gravely, 'and go on till you come to the end; then stop.' " (Lewis Carroll)

Before just rushing into this complex task of educating, the bigger picture has to be examined. What are the GOALS a teacher is trying to accomplish in paralegal education? Goals should articulate significant outcomes. (Recently, over 25 state legislatures have mandated that outcomes assessment be an integral part of educational programs.) The purpose of outcomes assessment is to measure the impact of the academic program on the students and to recommend improvements for programs, if necessary.

Six Goals of Paralegal Education

An excellent delineation of what paralegal education is trying to accomplish is expressed in Benjamin S. Bloom's, The Taxonomy of Educational Objectives. The author lists six cognitive skills that educators should help

12

students attain. The skills, listed in order of difficulty, start with *knowledge*, and progress through *comprehension, application, analysis, synthesis,* and *evaluation.*

Applying these skills to paralegal education, *knowledge* would consist of mastering the facts and principles of a subject. Example: Define the term "alternative dispute resolution." Proceeding to the next step of *comprehension*, the student would be expected to read an article written by U.S. Supreme Court Justice Sandra Day O'Connor and explain why Justice O'Connor believes that arbitration, a form of alternative dispute resolution, is a civil way to settle differences between individuals. The *application* step would require the student to use what has been learned and transfer to other situations. Example: Apply the principles of mediation in solving a real estate dispute between your next-door neighbor and you concerning planting of evergreen trees. *Analysis*, the fourth step, is concerned with the relationship between concepts. Example: Compare and contrast the principles of alternative dispute resolution with litigation. Another kind of cognitive skill is *synthesis*, putting together parts to form a whole. Example: What are the common threads between various methods of alternative dispute resolution. The pinnacle of cognitive reasoning is reached at the *evaluation* stage, the ability to make judgments. Example: Using the five-point criteria presented in James E. Jeans' video, "Litigation, The Art of Advocacy," critically evaluate Justice O'Connor's article on alternative dispute resolution.

Paralegal educators should be developing the higher cognitive skills of analysis, synthesis and evaluation, that is, the ability to think critically. One should not tell students to "Just Do It"; learning to think does not occur by osmosis. Rather, educators should help students question, challenge and avoid mere rote memorization.

Techniques to Achieve These Goals

Educators need to be aware of these six goals when preparing courses, formulating assignments, and conducting class discussion. For example, in order to review basic information for an upcoming *Introduction to Law* test, an instructor might spend part of the class conducting a "Jeopardy" type game in order to help students master basic material. (Instructor gives the definition of a legal term and the student determines what term is being described.) The goals of knowledge and comprehension are attained through this exercise. Example: Instructor -- "A formal way of discovering information in a litigation matter, which consists of a list of written questions asked by one party and answered by the other party under oath. Student -- "What are interrogatories."

On the other hand, if the instructor is trying to develop higher cognitive skills of application, analysis, synthesis, and evaluation in a *Legal Writing* course, the teacher might have students read the new Kansas legislation on capital punishment and respond in writing to the following questions:

1) identify assumptions of legislators who favored this legislation;
2) compare and contrast this law to Missouri's Death Penalty Statute; and
3) in your judgment, was former United States Supreme Court Justice Thurgood Marshall correct when he described the death penalty as a violation of the Eighth Amendment, which prohibits "cruel and unusual punishment?"

The ultimate purpose of any paralegal program is to help individuals think for themselves so they can assist in challenging tasks like drafting documents, interviewing clients, and analyzing legal and factual issues. Graduates of a paralegal program must "hit the ground running" in order to successfully meet the demands of their paralegal career.

CHAPTER THREE

The HOW of Paralegal Education
Methods of Instruction

Facilitator

Education must be <u>teacher-directed</u> and <u>student-centered</u>. The primary role of the teacher is to *facilitate* learning: to provide opportunities for students to master course content and skills. The days of the teacher acting as "Sage on the Stage" have been replaced by the teacher acting as "Guide on the Side."

Participation

A student cannot remain a spectator. Education demands participation. As an ancient learned person commented, "Show me, I remember; Involve me, I understand."

Ownership and Empowerment

While many roads can lead to education, the common denominator to successful teaching is <u>active learning</u>. Involvement of students in the education process has many advantages. The responsibility of learning is placed where it belongs: on the student's shoulders. Through this process of student-centered education, learners are empowered by possessing ownership in their education.

Lecture Style

The lecture style of teaching seems diametrically opposed to student-centered learning. However, this didactic approach can be a valuable way of presenting difficult material in an effective active learning method. Through various techniques, the teacher can prevent a lecture from becoming a mere dictation of complicated material. Nothing is as boring as a soliloquy that goes on, and on, and on....

Variety

When presenting the lesson, the instructor can move around the room and use different methods of conveying the information such as the blackboard and overhead transparencies. (The business community, who is an expert in commercial communication, reports that "people only retain ten percent of what they hear, 20 percent of what they see and 50 percent of what they hear and see.") Body language of an instructor, such as eye contact with students and facial gestures by the teacher, is important in a lecture presentation. Voice variance, especially the use of the "pregnant pause," can also be effective.

Socratic Method

The incorporation of the Socratic method, a teacher asking questions of students throughout the presentation, enhances a lecture. Example: When talking about discovery in the litigation process, ask why the Federal Rules of Civil Procedure allow certain material to be uncovered at this stage of litigation but the same material, such as information on insurance policies, is not allowed to be presented as evidence during the trial? Word of warning: Do not employ this technique so it becomes a "Grand Inquisition" session. If the instructor maintains a non-threatening classroom atmosphere, students are inclined to respond positively.

Examples and Illustrations

Another way to add spice to lectures is for the teacher to give multiple examples. An illustration can help link class material with reality. A discussion on preparation of a client for a deposition, elaborated on by a personal experience by either a student or teacher, is enlightening. Some students may also have served on jury duty and this valuable experience can be shared.

Devil's Advocate

To prevent a lecture from becoming a monologue, the teacher can interject a devil's advocate technique. Example: In a lecture on the federal court system, the instructor can question the wisdom of the Founding Fathers in establishing life-time appointment of federal judges. By raising doubts about some sacrosanct ideas, the teacher can ignite a lively discussion.

Culmination Activities

At the lecture's conclusion, students can form <u>cells</u>, or think-pairs, and compare lecture notes, helping one another clarify important points. Also each student can be asked to write a <u>One Minute Reaction Paper</u>, listing three to five main points from the lecture. Another reaction paper variation is to ask students to write one to three "clear as mud" points that the instructor made during the lecture, concepts that the students did not fully grasp. Class discussion can follow these exercises. Summary of key points at the conclusion of each class is essential. A reaction paper is only one way to accomplish this necessary function.

Active Learning

Many terms are used to describe active learning: co-operative education, shared inquiry, participatory education.... The essential factor is student involvement in his/her education.

Collaborative Learning
Interaction among students in working towards a common goal is collaborative learning. Helping students master a *team player approach* in solving problems must be an objective of a paralegal program. While self-reliant, self-directed paralegals are needed, a person must also excel in social interaction skills. A question that is frequently asked by an employer, when considering a paralegal student or graduate for employment, concerns an individual's abilities in group settings.

Group Discussion
Group discussion is a common type of learning through cooperation. To guarantee that this activity is worthwhile, proper preparation is needed:
1) from the first day of class, an open classroom atmosphere is present, that is, student participation is encouraged;
2) on a discussion day assign three people to a group in order to expose everyone to different viewpoints; and
3) within each group, designate roles: a moderator, a recorder

of information, and a reporter of the group's findings.
A time limit is imposed, with each group reaching closure
through a general report to the class. While group discussions
are in progress, the instructor should visit each group in an
observer's role. (An analysis of a case study in a group setting
can be effective.)

Case Study

Most textbooks provide hypothetical and real life cases.
Teachers can also develop other examples from contemporary
newspapers and magazines. In analyzing cases, three steps can
be followed:

1. Identify the disputes in the case,
2. State the legal principles, and
3. Explain your decision.

(A sample is included in Appendix II.)

Instructional Games

Another group activity is the use of instructional games, such
as role playing. Numerous types of mock client interviews
belong in this category. Example: Initial interview between a
paralegal and client concerning a personal injury matter.
Mock trials and mock appellant arguments are other effective
simulation exercises.

Using interactive video is another means of direct involvement
by students. In a typical interactive video scenario, the student
responds to situations on the screen. The computer program
reviews the student's performance and comments on the student choice. These presentations combine the power of the
computer and the realism of video to create authentic scenar-
ios. Example: ethical dilemma presented to students and

opportunity for individual to select best course of action from a given menu.

Debates

A debate on a controversial issue, such as regulation of parale-gals, involves student participation. The format can include student versus student or a group of students versus another group of students. However, students should perform exten-sive research before the debate in order to avoid a tendency towards "shared ignorance."

Panel Discussions

A panel discussion of practicing paralegals on life in the work world, including a question/answer period between panelists and students, is helpful. Panel discussions are an excellent way of having information communicated on practical aspects of attaining a job, such as tips on resume writing and inter-viewing by legal assistant administrators.

Guest Speakers

Guest speakers can offer specific valuable insights into classes. For example, it is helpful to have different attorney/paralegal teams come to specialized substantive classes like Family Law, Workers' Compensation, and Bankruptcy in order to share their expertise. Time should be allowed for a question/answer peri-od between speakers and students.

Field Trips

Field Trips to the Register of Deed office for a Real Estate class or to a detention facility for a Criminal Law class are memorable experiences for students. A beneficial visit for Administrative Law students is to an agency hearing. Also, students gain insights by visiting a court to observe actual proceedings.

Student Reports

<u>Individual or group oral reports</u>, which incorporate multimedia presentations of charts/diagrams, video tapes, slides, overhead projections, and computer demonstrations, are effective <u>active learning</u> techniques. Example: Several students could explain major parts of a trial by using short excerpts from videos like <u>My Cousin Vinny</u>, <u>A Few Good Men</u>, and <u>Twelve Angry Men</u>. Also, old reruns of <u>Leave It To Beaver</u> can be used to explain concepts such as the attractive nuisance doctrine. (Example: Beaver trespasses in order to climb a neighbor's 20-foot ladder, which is propped against the house.)

Interviews

Conducting <u>interviews</u> and reporting the findings to the class is another excellent active learning method. Phone or personal interviews by an individual student with a working paralegal are beneficial in helping students learn about the profession.

Most paralegals are flattered if a student asks them about their profession. However, to make sure that an individual does not mind visiting with a student, it is a good idea to formulate a list of volunteers. Names can be gathered from alumni lists, advisory boards, and members of local legal assistant organizations.

Demonstrations

Paralegal students are influenced by the exciting technology revolution within today's legal profession. A way to involve students, as well as keep them up-to-date, is to encourage class demonstrations of specialized legal software and hardware by individual students. Also, the use of computers to readily retrieve and reconfigure vast amounts of electronically-stored information should be demonstrated in class as well as employed by students for completion of individual research assignments.

Other Active Learning Strategies
Other active learning methods are drafting of *voir dire* questions; preparing discovery documents; developing flow charts of the litigation process, and of a state's worker's compensation and/or bankruptcy procedures; and writing a letter to a client concerning the status of his/her case. "Students must talk about what they are learning, write about it, relate it to past experiences and apply it to their daily lives."

Non-Traditional Student

Student-centered, teacher-directed education is worthwhile for any type of learner but is especially helpful to the non-traditional, older than 25 years old student. Because older students have a broader experience base to draw upon, teaching methods should allow for frequent class participation and acknowledge and use students' backgrounds through active learning. Older students are goal-directed but concerned about re-entering school. They fear that they no longer possess the abilities they once had and cannot successfully compete. A supportive and relaxed climate in the classroom will help counter these concerns. Further, the designing of short-term assignments so students receive early and frequent feed-back is important. The use of hand-outs to reinforce major points and summarizing points at the end of a lecture assists non-traditional students. Finally these students demand their "money's worth." They have a <u>practical orientation to learning</u> and want the classroom material to be correct and up-to-date. <u>Field trips</u>, <u>guest speakers</u>, and <u>interviews</u> assist in a pragmatic approach.

Traditional Student

Teachers should be aware that <u>traditional</u> students are more hesitant about making class contributions. Establishing a non-intimidating atmosphere, where students are encouraged to participate, is essential. Also, bringing traditional students into class discussions by asking them to respond to easier questions at first, will build confidence. Example: After spending a class period discussing the U. S. Supreme Court, ask a reticent student what is one thing he/she could share with a student who was absent concerning important material covered during the class. Another technique is to designate slow-to-participate students as reporters in group discussions.

Standards

Finally, each student deserves to be challenged. Even though the class is composed of students with various backgrounds and abilities, students object to any practice of "dumbing down."
Acquiescing to lower standards is an insult. Most students rise to a teacher's highest expectation. Quality education should be a hallmark of every paralegal program.

CHAPTER FOUR

The HOW of Paralegal Education
<u>First Day of Class</u>

First Day

The saying, "first impressions create lasting impressions" is true in regard to the beginning of a semester. The <u>tone</u> for the next months is set by this first class. A "meet and dismiss" procedure is not recommended for this first day. It is important to establish a climate of learning immediately.

Self Introduction

The classroom atmosphere should be comfortable. A way of encouraging this openness is by a teacher beginning with <u>self-introduction</u>. A short autobiographical sketch is appropriate and can comprise both personal and professional backgrounds. Including several comments about a person's educational philosophy, as well as mention of why the individual is teaching this specific course, are also beneficial. A teacher's vitality and excitement should permeate this first session.

Roll

To become acquainted with students, <u>class roll</u> should be taken at the first class and throughout the semester. Knowing the attendance record of individual students can be valuable information, especially if the student encounters some academic problems. A teacher should also be cognizant of any college policy in regard to tying grades to attendance.

Textbook Review

A review of the textbook(s) is an important activity. Highlighting unique features of the book, such as glossary, case studies, and charts, can be included in the overview. Time can also be spent on a specific "walk-through" of an individual chapter, noting organization and features like definition of terms, chapter questions, and summary paragraphs. The suggestion that a student read the chapter material at least twice, once before class and once after the presentation, should be stressed. Caution: Avoid criticizing the text during the course to students; however, if an instructor feels that the book is inadequate, that opinion should be conveyed to the proper administrator so that the book can be re-evaluated for future use. Also, teachers should use the text(s). Students do not appreciate buying expensive books that are used infrequently during the course. Teachers should be able to explain basic book concepts <u>and</u> expand on these important principles during class.

Class Syllabus

An important document is the <u>class syllabus</u>. It is a road map of the course. Since it constitutes an agreement between the faculty member and student, it should be distributed and reviewed during this first class. Before drafting a course syllabus for the first time, the instructor should check to see if there are any specific written school guidelines, any sample syllabi available, and whether there is a previous teacher of the course that the instructor could visit. Most syllabi will include information about

⊗ the instructor

⊗ the course

⊗ class schedule

⊗ textbook

⊗ evaluation and grading scale

Specific areas that should be addressed are policies on attendance, test make-up and late assignment. Again, teachers need to check that their rules do not contradict any general rules of the institution. (A sample syllabus is included in Appendix III.)

Learning Styles

A discussion of different *types of learning styles* is appropriate on the first day. A basic principle of education is that all students can learn but it is done at various rates and in different ways. One break-down of student learning styles classifies four means of mastering materials:

the accommodator is a person who is open to new ideas, and learns by trial and error;

the diverger is a person who has creative, imaginative traits, and learns by listening and sharing ideas;

the applicator is a person who arrives at conclusions through deductive reasoning/logic, and learns by testing theories and experimenting;

the assimilator is a person who abstracts, an inductive type, and learns through lectures and reading.

Not surprisingly, teachers are inclined to teach according to the way they learn. In the role of teacher,

the <u>accommodator</u> likes variety in instructional methods;

the <u>diverger</u> likes discussion and group work;

the <u>applicator</u> likes practical applications and hands-on activities;

the <u>assimilator</u> likes to transmit knowledge, such as detailed facts in a sequential order.

Teachers should try to incorporate each learning/teaching style in their course.

Student Introductions

A final way of conducting a beneficial first class is to use a <u>get-acquainted activity</u> with the students. Some possible methods are to

a) ask students to pair off and spend 3-5 minutes interviewing each other and have each person introduce his/her partner to the class;

b) use a personal scavenger hunt to have people meet, answer questions, and mix; some sample questions to use:

1) Find a classmate who has a relative or friend who is a practicing legal assistant;

2) Name a classmate who has worked in one of the non-traditional paralegal areas, such as banking, insurance or real estate;

3) Discover a classmate whose has served as a juror, witness, plaintiff or defendant at a trial by jury;

　　c) ask students to introduce themselves by giving one or two informational pieces that people will remember about them, a "something special" approach.

Transitions

Wow---one teaching day down and many more to come! What about all those remaining classes? To begin the other classes well is also an important task. Two methods can be used in approaching these classes:

　　a) the social transition technique, or
　　b) the academic warm-up method.

Using the <u>social transition</u> technique, the teacher eases into the course material by visiting with the class for two or three minutes about general matters: articles in the latest school newspaper or reaction of students to a current movie like "Philadelphia."

Another variation of this general transitional technique is to have each student assigned a date on which he/she is responsible to open the class with a one-minute current event report. Good sources of information can be found in the <u>Wall Street Journal</u>, <u>American Bar Association Journal</u>, or <u>Legal Assistant Today</u>.

The <u>academic approach</u> focuses on "setting the stage" for the material about to be considered during the class. Numerous methods can be used to implement this approach:

　　⊗ showing a cartoon or slide about the material,

　　⊗ telling an anecdote connected to the material,

　　⊗ eliciting student questions about the material, writing the questions on the board, and answering the questions during the class,

⊗ giving an ungraded "pre-test" on the material, using a true/false format,

⊗ reviewing the last class material in relation to the new material, or

⊗ presenting a problem to the students concerning the new material and asking their reaction. (If discussing adoption, present the "Baby Jessica" case. A consideration of the "Baby M" case is an excellent way to begin a discussion concerning a surrogate.)

CHAPTER FIVE

The HOW of Paralegal Education
Methods of Evaluation

Introduction

Another challenging aspect of teaching deals with student evaluation. It is necessary that the instructor have a firm grasp of the general purpose of student evaluation.Also, an instructor needs to know the various kinds of tests and different ways to administer examinations.

An instructor who believes that formal evaluation should be a "gotcha" approach, needs to rethink the teaching/learning process. What a powerful difference it makes if teachers really believe that <u>every</u> <u>student</u> <u>can</u> <u>succeed</u>. Testing is not a "sorting and selecting" process. It is a means of allowing students to demonstrate their competencies.

An open-book examination is appropriate in certain circumstances. A test should not be an exercise to determine which student has the best memory. A paralegal needs to know where to discover information and to know what the information means. In some situations, such as a litigation course, students should be allowed to use the <u>Federal Rules of Civil Procedure</u> during a test. It is more important that a student can apply and analyze the rules than it is to have them committed to memory.

Test Recommendations

Some test pointers are:

    a) give more than mid-term and final examinations each semester, (frequent feedback to students is beneficial)

    b) give a test within the first three weeks of the semester so students are given an early opportunity to synthesize the material,

    c) return tests at the next class,

    d) review returned tests at the end of the next class.
(It is important that students are given an opportunity to review tests. A few students like to argue "ad nauseam" about each point and waste time for the other students. To counter this tendency, 15 minutes can be set aside at the end of the class to distribute and discuss the test. If students want to review the matter further, they can be encouraged to see the instructor after class or during office hours. It is amazing how few choose these options!)

Construction of a test is an important task. Some general guidelines are to:

    ⊗ provide clear directions;

    ⊗ ask questions directly, avoiding trick questions;

    ⊗ allot a reasonable amount of time for the test;

    ⊗ provide a testing environment; and

    ⊗ design a test that can be accurately scored.

Written Tests

There are five basic types of written test items:

⊗ true/false;

⊗ matching;

⊗ multiple-choice;

⊗ short-answer; and

⊗ essay.

If the teacher is trying to challenge the students' higher cognitive abilities of application, analysis, synthesis, and evaluation, the last three types of test items are useful.

Multiple-Choice Test

When constructing multiple-choice questions, provide at least four possible answers. Each one should be plausible but only one is clearly the best answer. Try to keep the choices about the same length.

Sample Question (*Directions: Choose the best answer--one point for each correct answer.*)

A reply to a counterclaim is a

a) defendant's answer to an affirmative defense,

b) defendant's answer to a cross-claim

c) plaintiff's answer to a cross-claim

d) plaintiff's answer to a defendant's answer.

Short-Answer Test

Responses to short-answer items can range from one word to a few sentences. Well-formulated short answer questions avoid "too general" and "too trivial" questions.

Sample Question (*Directions: Question is worth 5 points.*)

Deborah entered into a contract to supply 15 lemon cakes to <u>Only Desserts</u>, a gourmet food store and caterer that planned to serve the cakes at a wedding dinner. The contract provided that Deborah had to deliver the lemon cakes to <u>Only Desserts</u> by 5:00 pm on March 1, 1994 and that "time is of the essence." What is the significance of the words, "Time is of the essence?"

Essay Test

<u>Essay</u> <u>items</u> are extended short answers and consist of several paragraphs. While essay tests are fairly easy to construct, they are more difficult to grade because of subjective factors. Several ways to lessen this problem are to prepare a model answer before grading any paper and to do one quick read-through of all papers before grading the papers. If the test consists of several essays, grade all of one essay answer first on each paper rather than all essays on one student's paper. When writing an essay test, limit the problem so that everyone who reads the question will derive the same meaning from it. A good question asks for specific answers.

<u>Sample</u> <u>Question</u> *(Answer each part of the essay question. Each subsection is worth 5 points. Total points are 15 points.)*

Frank, a resident of Kansas City, Kansas, is furious. He just lost a $100,000 breach of contract suit against Dimitri's Greek Restaurant. The case was decided at a Kansas district court. Frank has informed his attorney that he wants her to take the case "all the way to the U.S. Supreme Court," if necessary.

a) Discuss a legal issue which Frank could use in order to appeal the case to a Kansas Appellate

Court.

b) Can Frank bypass the Kansas Appellate process and have his case immediately heard by the U.S Supreme Court? (Explain your answer)

c) Could Frank have originally started this case in a federal trial court rather than in the state system? (Explain your answer)

An interesting variation of this three-part essay question would be to allow the students the option to choose two of the three questions to answer. Another technique is to give students three to five possible essay questions in a review session several days before the test. On the test day, the teacher selects one or two questions for examination purpose.

Small Group Testing

The way that students take examinations can vary. Small group testing or tandem testing is used in some classroom settings. This collaborative testing can be applied to <u>multiple-choice</u> tests:

1) each student takes the test individually;

2) students form their own groups or assemble in assigned groups;

3) each group takes the test together;

4) each group submits its answers for preliminary scoring. The teacher grades and tells the groups <u>how many</u> questions are incorrect <u>but not which questions</u> are incorrect;

5) the group reviews its answer and may alter its initial answer for final grading;

6) the group submits tests for final grading;

7) the instructor may record individual scores and

group scores or some combination of each.

There are certain implications for designing a group test. The number of questions should be reduced to allow for discussion. Any type of question may be used but essay responses take more time. Three people are recommended for a group.

Another group variation is to ask students to:
1) select two other class members;
2) study individually and meet to study, if desired;
3) answer the test *solo* first;
4) attempt to reach consensus;
5) turn in individual answer sheets and/or one group sheet; (teacher can record the higher grade.)

A common complaint of students is that some instructors teach one way but test another. To avoid this problem, the teacher should have a crystal-clear idea of the purpose of the test. Secondly, adequate review for the test is essential. During the class before the examination, students can spend time on review. One method is for the teacher, through interaction with students, to list major content areas for the upcoming test on the board. Students can then form small groups. Each group is assigned one content area and formulates possible exam questions concerning that material. Each group shares their questions orally with the other students before the class ends.

Written Assignments

A teacher can also employ a positive attitude towards grading any written work: the pencil approach rather than the red ink method. Many teachers collect an assignment, grade the work, and then give feedback concerning the work. The steps should be reversed: give a reaction to the paper first, allow the student to revise it, and then give the final grade to the work.

By employing a safety net approach, teachers acknowledge that students are not automatons, mastering knowledge and skills in robotic fashion. Competency is not determined by an arbitrary schedule but by individual progress.

POSTSCRIPT

on

Strategies and Tips for Paralegal Educators

The author has presented some new, old, and recycled ideas in these pages. Should you try any of them? Isn't there something about "don't fix it if it ain't broken?" But isn't there also a saying about **"there is no such thing as standing still, for if we are not moving ahead, we are falling behind."**

Teaching is a dynamic profession and we must be risk-takers. In baseball, **"runners cannot reach second base until they take their foot off first."** We need to experience the thrill of reaching second base, third base, and home through our classroom experiences!

Have a great time at the ball park!

APPENDICES

CLASS OUTLINE

THE COURT SYSTEM

I. Definition of Court

II. Kinds of Courts
   A. Trial
      1. General
      2. Specific
         a. Civil
         b. Criminal

   B. Appellate Courts
      1. General
      2. Specific
         a. Court of Appeals
         b. Supreme Court

III. System of Courts
   A. Type of Courts
      1. Federal
      2. State
      3. Local
         a. County/City
         b. Small Claims Court

   B. Jurisdiction
      1. Subject Matter
      2. Personal
      3. Other

IV. Adversarial System
   A. Definition

B. Parties

V. Trial Procedure
   A. Pleading

   B. Discovery

   C. Trial

   D. Post Trial

VI. Alternative Dispute Resolutions
   A. Definition

   B. Types

Introduction to Law course
Text: <u>Understanding the Law</u>, Carper, West Publication
Chapter 3: "The Court System"

CASE STUDY

(Article excerpted from a newspaper)

Article: "A Deadly Aim"

Karen Wood, the mother of twin baby girls, was killed in her own backyard. It was during Maine's hunting season and she was mistaken for a deer.

The death of the 37-year-old bank loan officer, who, with her husband, Kevin, had recently moved to a town near Bangor, touched off an extraordinary legal debate over the rights of hunters and citizens.

Hunting accidents occur frequently, but the death of Karen Wood was different. She was in her own backyard in a residential neighborhood when she was shot.

The Grand Jury found that the incident was not indictable: even involuntary manslaughter, the accidental, negligent killing of another, was ruled out. Karen's husband believes the decision comes from the fact that he and his family were newcomers in a close-knit community. Some resident blamed Karen for not wearing an orange garment during hunting season. The hunter, Donald Rogerson, 46, told authorities he thought he saw a deer in the scope of his high-powered rifle. He quickly fired two shots. One hit a tree; the other pierced Mrs. Wood's heart. Authorities later told her husband there was no evidence of a deer in the vicinity--no furs, no tracks.

Rogerson, a popular grocer and scoutmaster, said he didn't realize he was hunting near houses. But Karen's husband says that it was a relatively short distance between Karen and the hunter, who killed her with his power rifle, about 63 yards. Hunters are supposed to stay at least 100 yards from all residential buildings.

Meanwhile, Karen's family filed CIVIL SUIT. Mr. Wood settled the wrongful-death suit for $122,000.

QUESTIONS:
1. Identify the dispute(s) in the case,
2. State the legal principle(s), and
3. Explain your decision -- Is Mr. Rogerson and the Grand Jury correct or is Mr. Wood correct?

Introduction to Law course
Text: <u>Understanding the Law</u>, Carper, West Publication

JOHNSON COUNTY COMMUNITY COLLEGE
Course Syllabus
Business Technology and Computer Instruction Division
INTRODUCTION TO LAW
PL 121 04
Fall 1994

INSTRUCTOR INFORMATION :

Anita Tebbe
Office Phone: 469-8500, ext 3184
Office OCB 255-B

COURSE INFORMATION:

CREDIT HOURS: 3

PREREQUISITE(S): None

REQUIRED TEST(S): Understanding the Law, Carper et al., St. Paul, MN:
                   West Publishing Company, 1991.

SUPPLEMENTAL BOOKS: None

SUPPLIES: None

CAVEATS: None

COURSE DESCRIPTION:

Upon successful completion of this course, the student should be able to
explain the major substantive and procedural aspects of law. Some areas
covered include contract law, family law, property law, business law, estates
and probate law and criminal law. The course is available to students with a
general interest in law and required of students seeking admission to the
Paralegal Program.

COURSE OBJECTIVES:

Upon successful completion of this course, the student should be able to:

1. Explain the structure of the federal, Kansas and Missouri court systems.

2. Identify the jurisdictional requirements and types of cases handled by the federal and state court systems.

3. Explain the selection of judges.

4. Explain the appellate process of the federal and Kansas court systems.

5. Explain the Small Claims procedure.

6. Differentiate between Chapter 60 and Chapter 61 actions in Kansas courts.

7. Identify the functions of various public agencies that operate in the legal environment, such as prosecutors, public defenders and legal aid, at the federal, state and local levels.

8. Describe the functions of various government agencies and their relationship to the legal environment.

9. Explain the functions and interrelationships of the legislative, judicial and executive branches of government.

10. Locate statutory and case laws.

11. Explain the administrative law process.

12. Describe the lawyer's function in the legal system and the costs of legal representation.

13. Explain the four stages of civil litigation: pleadings, discovery, trial and appeal.

14. Identify the elements of a crime.

15. Utilize the Kansas criminal statutes.

16. Explain the basic elements of a contract.

17. Identify statutory contractual requirements.

18. Explain the three main types of business ownership: sole proprietorship, partnership and corporation.

19. Differentiate between an agent and an independent contractor.

20. List the requirements for a valid marriage.

21. Explain the process of termination of the marital relationship.

22. Differentiate between real and personal property.

23. Explain the concepts of intestate succession and testate succession.

24. List the steps to follow in probating an estate.

25. Differentiate between the types of tortious claims.

COURSE REQUIREMENTS:

All students should take tests and turn in assignments at the time they are scheduled. In the event of illness or an emergency situation on a test date, the instructor must be notified prior to or immediately after the class session. Make-up tests will be given in the testing center provided the proper notification has been given to the instructor. All make-up tests must be taken prior to the next class meeting. Any late assignment will be assessed a penalty of 5 points for each weekday that it is late.

If you must be absent, please arrange to have another student pick up handouts and announcements for you. It is your responsibility to stay advised of any schedule change in the course syllabus and to obtain class notes. It is not necessary to contact the instructor when you are absent on a date when there are no tests or assignments due.

SCHOOL POLICIES:

The last date to withdraw from a 16-week course is Nov. 15, 1994. Please note that if you elect to withdraw from a course, you must do so through the Admissions Office.

Any student who has a disability that may prevent him/her from fully demonstrating his/her abilities should contact me personally as soon as possible to discuss reasonable accommodations necessary to complete the course requirements.

1.   Tests - 200 points

      1st Test: Chapters 1, 2, 3   = 50 points
      2nd Test: Chapters 4, 5, 6, 11   = 50 points
      3rd Test: Chapters 8, 9, 10, 14   = 50 points
      4th Test: Chapters 7, 12, 13, 15   = 50 points

2.   Projects - 100 points

      A. Court Visit   - 50 points
      B. Current Event Report   - 50 points

COURT VISIT:

Point Value: 50

Date Due: 11/1

1.   Visit any court in this area and observe the proceedings for at least one hour. You may go to a Kansas or Missouri state court, municipal court, or federal court. (For most of you the Johnson County District Court in Olathe will be most convenient.)

2.   Write a 2-4 page paper (double-spaced) in which you discuss the proceeding you observed. Your paper must include the following information:

    a.   The name of the court by state, district, division, etc.

    b.   The name of the judge and the attorneys involved

    c.   The name of the case (or cases) you heard; identify the plaintiff and the defendant or other parties involved

    d.   The type of case or proceeding you observed

    e.   Your impression of the proceeding, including the atmosphere and environment in the courtroom, the demeanor of the people who were present, the effectiveness of the people who participated, and your overall reaction to the manner in which the proceeding was handled.

    f.   Be prepared to talk about your court visit with the class. You must make an oral presentation to receive full credit for the assignment. (Ten points will be deducted for omitting the oral presentation.)

CURRENT EVENT REPORT: You will sign up for one of the follow presentations:

1st Presentation: Courts - Tuesday, Sept. 13
2nd Presentation: Torts, Crime, Contracts and Motor Vehicles - Tuesday, Oct. 18
3rd Presentation: Family Law, Wills, Employees' Rights, Small Business - Tuesday, Nov. 15
4th Presentation: Administrative Law, Attorney-Client, Renters and Homeowners - Tuesday, Dec. 6

Directions: After you sign up for one of the presentations, you will find a current article, one from January 1994 or later, which deals with your subject matter. Locate an article from the newspaper or current news magazine, such as *Time, Newsweek, Business Week,* etc. No presenter will discuss the same specific topic as any other presenter. You may change your specific topic up to the time you give your oral presentation as long as no other presenter has chosen that particular topic.

Presentation: Each presenter will deliver an oral presentation on the chosen article for 5 minutes. Your discussion should center on the following three points:

1. Discussion of facts   20 points
2. Explanation of legal issue(s)   20 points
3. Comment on relevance of
     article to course   10 points
              TOTAL POINTS   50 points

TENTATIVE COURSE SCHEDULE:

Tuesday Aug. 23   Introduction to Course
                       Chapter 1: Introduction to Law

Tuesday Aug. 30   Chapter 2: Our Constitution

Tuesday Sep. 6   Chapter 3: The Court System

Tuesday Sep. 13   Test: Chapters 1, 2, 3
                       First Presentation: Courts

Tuesday Sep. 20   Chapter 4: Crime

Tuesday Sep. 27   Chapter 5: Torts

Tuesday Oct. 4   Chapter 6: Contracts

Tuesday Oct. 11   Chapter 11: Motor Vehicle

Tuesday Oct. 18   Test: Chapters 4, 5, 6, 11
                       Second Presentation: Torts,
                       Crime, Contracts and Motor Vehicles

Tuesday Oct. 25   Chapter 8:   Family Law

Tuesday Nov. 1   Chapter 14: Wills
                       Court Report Due

Tuesday Nov. 8   Chapter 9: Employees' Rights
                       Chapter 10: Small Business

Tuesday Nov. 15   Test: Chapter 8, 9, 10, 14
                       Third Presentation: Family Law,
                       Wills, Employees' Rights and Small Business

Tuesday Nov. 22   Chapter 7: Administrative Law
                       Chapter 15: Attorney-Client

Tuesday Nov. 29   Chapter 12: Renters
                       Chapter 13: Homeowners

Tuesday Dec. 6   Fourth Presentation: Administrative Law,
                       Attorney-Client, Renters and Homeowners

Tuesday Dec. 13   Final Examination: Chapter 7, 12, 13, 15

Paralegal Program Directors
YOU CAN PURCHASE COPIES OF THIS MANUAL for all of your instructors.

Any instructor who adopts a West paralegal textbook can receive a free copy of this manual. Additional copies are available for only:

$11.46 each

(price subject to change without notice)

To order your copies, fill out the coupon below and send with payment to:
West Publishing Corporation
Attn: COP Department
620 Opperman Drive
P.O. Box 64833
St. Paul, MN 55164-1803

To order by phone, call 1-800-340-9378. Please have a credit card or West account number on hand when you make your call. Allow 6-8 weeks for delivery.

Please send ___ copies of ***Strategies and Tips for Paralegal Educators*** (ISBN: 0-314-04971-1) at $11.46 each plus my state and local tax for a total of $_____ .

Order subject to approval of vendor. Applicable local tax to be added. Price subject to change without notice.

Mail to:

Name: _____

School: _____

Department: _____

Address: _____

City: _____

State: _____

Zip:_____
